FAITH, HOPE, AND LOVE

FAITH, HOPE, AND LOVE

The Ecumenical Trio of Virtues

Geoffrey Wainwright

BAYLOR UNIVERSITY PRESS

Cover Design by Savanah Landerholm

Library of Congress Cataloging-in-Publication Data

Wainwright, Geoffrey, 1939–
  Faith, hope, and love : the ecumenical trio of virtues / Geoffrey
Wainwright.
  72 pages cm
  Includes bibliographical references.
  ISBN 978-1-4813-0085-8 (pbk. : alk. paper)
1. Theological virtues. 2. Faith. 3. Hope—Religious aspects—
Christianity. 4. Love—Religious aspects—Christianity. 5. Bap-
tism. 6. Lord's prayer. 7. Lord's Supper. 8. Worship. I. Title.
  BV4635.W24 2014
  241'.4--dc23

                    2013045463

Printed in the United States of America on acid-free paper with a
minimum of 30% post-consumer waste recycled content.

CONTENTS
∞

PREFACE
ɛɔ

It was for me a high honor to be invited to give at Baylor University in October 2012 the annual Leo and Gloriana Parchman Endowed Lectures. My name would thus be attached to the long and much admired list of scholarly and churchly predecessors.

My lectures took place on October 9 and 10 in the Paul W. Powell Chapel of Baylor University's George W. Truett Theological Seminary, where they received careful and appreciative attention.

From the start my texts were conceived and composed with a view to oral delivery and aural reception. That style continues to characterize the present publication, which thus gives—both to the original hearers and to new readers—visual access to my thoughts on the announced subject: "Faith, Hope, and Love" as the "Ecumenical Trio of Virtues."

My thanks are due to all those at Baylor who offered me a personal welcome, generous hospitality, and stimulating conversation—all of which surrounded my formal presentations. In particular I mention Dr. Brian Brewer, assistant professor of Christian theology at Truett Seminary, who served my practical and administrative needs in a collegial context and manner.

Now at the moment of this publication, I thank particularly Dr. Carey Newman, director of Baylor University Press, as well as Jordan Rowan Fannin, who has shown her respectful editorial care to my text.

Geoffrey Wainwright
The Divinity School
Duke University

INTRODUCTION
&

Faith, hope, and love: the ecumenical trio of virtues. That densely phrased title might benefit from a little preliminary unpacking.

We may begin with St. Paul's First Letter to the Corinthians, and the thirteenth chapter. For many long years in Britain, that was among the favorite passages of Scripture set to be learned both by Sunday school pupils and even by the children in day school. We used, of course, the Authorized Version of Scripture, the King James Bible. You, too, may remember how the passage began: "Though I speak with the tongues of men and of angels, and have not charity, I am become as sounding brass, or a tinkling cymbal. And though I have the gift of prophecy, and understand all mysteries, and all knowledge; and though I have all faith, so that I could remove mountains, and have not charity, I am nothing." And on it goes: charity "beareth all things, believeth all things, hopeth all things, endureth all things. Charity never faileth"—until we reach the last verse of the chapter: "And now abideth faith, hope, charity, these three; but the greatest of these is charity." Faith, hope, and charity: the linguistic nuances have shifted in recent years, and so instead of "charity" we now say "love."

Faith, hope, and love: I am calling them a "trio"; but that may sound too simplistic. So let me offer another Pauline passage, where all three do indeed figure but are intertwined within a more complex argument. I am thinking of the first five verses of the fifth chapter in the Letter to the Romans, reading this time from the Revised Standard Version of the Bible:

> Therefore, since we are justified by FAITH, we have peace with God through our Lord Jesus Christ. Through him we have obtained access to this grace in which we stand, and we rejoice in our HOPE of sharing the glory of God. More than that, we rejoice in our sufferings, knowing that suffering produces endurance [*hupomonē*], and endurance produces character [*dokimē*], and character produces HOPE, and HOPE does not disappoint us, because God's LOVE has been poured into our hearts through the Holy Spirit which has been given to us.

Notice the connections made there among our three terms of faith, hope, and love, with which "grace," "endurance," "character," and "glory" are also connected. Notice also the

discreet trinitarianism of that passage, and its implied chris-
tocentrism: those two key features will be found to belong to
our "virtues" both as to the "content" and as to the "act" of all
three—faith, hope, and love. I shall also be finding help in the
Letter to the Romans to make respective matches between our
three ecumenical virtues and three rites of the Church that
were instituted by the Lord himself: FAITH matched with holy
baptism; HOPE matched with the Lord's Prayer; LOVE matched
with the Lord's Supper.

By title I am speaking of a trio of "virtues." In broad human
understanding, a virtue is a good habit of action, and a classical
list includes temperance, fortitude, justice, and prudence as
"cardinal" virtues. Christian teaching distinguishes and highlights our three—faith, hope, and love—as directly infused
gifts from God—"charisms"—to which we are called and
which we are expected to exercise. Appropriately, they are
designated "theological virtues."

Faith, hope, and love: I call them an "ecumenical" trio.
By that I mean that they are bestowed on all individual Christians and on the communities—large or small—in which they
gather. More especially, I mean that the exercise of those virtues has been seen as the route to the attainment of that cor-
porate unity toward which the "Ecumenical Movement" in our
time points and works. Already in its decree on ecumenism
the Second Vatican Council declared the historical foundation and the theological principle: "After being lifted up on

3

the cross and glorified, the Lord Jesus poured forth the Spirit whom he had promised, and through whom he has called and gathered together the people of the New Covenant, which is the Church, into a unity of faith, hope and love."[1]

Meeting at Porto Alegre (Brazil) in the year 2006, the Ninth Assembly of the World Council of Churches (WCC) unanimously adopted an ecclesiological text prepared for it by the Faith and Order Commission of the WCC: "Called to be the One Church: An invitation to the churches to renew their commitment to the search for unity and to deepen their dialogue." One particular passage is of special interest in connection with our trio of faith, hope, and love:

> The life of the Church as new life in Christ is *one*. Yet it is built up through different charismata and ministries. . . . Some differences express God's grace and goodness; they must be discerned in God's grace through the Holy Spirit. Other differences divide the Church; these must be overcome through the Spirit's gifts of FAITH, HOPE, and LOVE so that separation and exclusion do not have the last word. . . . God calls his people in love to discernment and renewal on the way to the fullness of koinonia.[2]

As an exercise in "mutual accountability" and "mutual responsibility," the churches are invited to "engage in the hard task of giving a candid account of the relation of their own faith and order to the faith and order of other churches." The churches "are called to address recurrent matters in fresh, more pointed ways," being "challenged to recognize areas for renewal in their own lives, and new opportunities to deepen relations with those of other traditions." Finally, "Noting the progress made in the ecumenical movement, we encourage our churches to continue on this arduous yet joyous path, trusting in God the Father, Son and Holy Spirit, whose grace transforms our struggles for unity into the fruits of communion." Each member church was called upon to respond to the text and the series of questions it posed concerning the churches and their mutual relations, expecting the responses to be coordinated by the Faith and Order Commission with a view to the Tenth Assembly of the WCC in 2013.[3]

Notice especially that the divisions among Christians and their communities are to be overcome "through the Spirit's gifts of faith, hope, and love so that separation and exclusion do not have the last word."

My plan in these lectures is to examine those three gifts of the Spirit as they are received and exercised in three focal acts of Christian worship, with a view especially to their ecclesially unifying energy. I aim to show how our understanding and observance of three rites or practices instituted by the Lord himself can move us toward unity in faith, hope, and love. I shall match FAITH with HOLY BAPTISM; I shall match HOPE with the LORD'S PRAYER; I shall match LOVE with the LORD'S SUPPER.

While addressing largely an audience of Baptists (with whom I have also talked in the past), I shall speak as a life-long Methodist: I was baptized at the age of six weeks in our Blucher Street church in Barnsley, Yorkshire; I am intellectually and aesthetically shaped by the Wesley brothers, the often prosaic John and the always poetic Charles; and I have been an ordained minister of the Methodist Church of Great Britain since 1967. Ecumenically, I have multilateral experience, especially through the Faith and Order Commission of the WCC, where I remember the contributions of Baptist members; and I have bilateral experience, particularly through the dialogue between the World Methodist Council and the Roman Catholic Church, whose Joint Commission I chaired on the Methodist side from 1986 to 2011; and I am aware of the "conversations" between representatives of the Baptist World Alliance and the Pontifical Council for Promoting Christian Unity.

The first virtue in my trio is "faith," and I may perhaps be allowed to prepare the way by a gift from Methodism to the wider Church in the shape of a hymn by Charles Wesley, "Spirit of faith, come down":

Spirit of faith, come down,
Reveal the things of God;
And make to us the Godhead known,
And witness with the blood.

'Tis Thine the blood to apply,
And give us eyes to see
Who did for every sinner die
Hath surely died for me.

No man can truly say
That Jesus is the Lord,
Unless Thou take the veil away,
And breathe the living word;
Then, only then, we feel
Our interest in His blood,
And cry with joy unspeakable:
Thou art my Lord, my God!

O that the world might know
The all-atoning Lamb!
Spirit of faith, descend, and show
The virtue of His name;
The grace which all may find,
The saving power impart;
And testify to all mankind,
And speak in every heart.

Inspire the living faith,
Which whosoe'er receives,
The witness in himself he hath,
And consciously believes;

The faith that conquers all,
And doth the mountain move,
And saves whoe'er on Jesus call,
And perfects them in love.[4]

Faith I will expound in relation to holy baptism. Or should I expound holy baptism in relation to faith? Ideally, I would like to set the two in mutual, interactive relationship.

FAITH AND HOLY BAPTISM
ଈୠ

Inevitably we must begin with historical and theological controversy.

Those whom we now call—and who call themselves—"Baptists" emerge around the time of the Reformation. Their reading of Western Christendom showed them a multitudinous Church whose failings could be attributed—at least in part—to the indiscriminate practice of baptism.

The defenders of the centuries-old practice of administering baptism to the infant children of Christians nicknamed their opponents "*Ana*-baptist" for presuming to "baptize again" such people if and when, in later years, they came to a "personal" faith that they could profess. It was the common teaching that a person might properly receive baptism only once. Of course, the "Ana-baptists" considered that the baptism they administered was in fact the unique baptism, so that they might more fittingly be called "Baptist"—without the "Ana." The disparity between the two camps came to be formulated in terms of "infant baptism" and "believer baptism." Along the way, we shall come to ecumenical attempts to reconcile the two positions, or at least to accommodate them, paying particular attention to the chapter "Baptism" in the so-called Lima text of 1982, *Baptism, Eucharist and Ministry* (*BEM*), and developments in that process; but we will start with the beginnings of baptism.[5]

The last verses of Matthew's Gospel present the risen Lord as instituting baptism, so Baptists are quite correct to term the rite a "dominical ordinance": Jesus came and said to them (that is, to the "eleven disciples"), "All authority in heaven and on earth has been given to me. Go therefore and make disciples of all nations, baptizing them in the name of the Father and of the Son and of the Holy Spirit, teaching them to observe all that I have commanded you; and lo, I am with you always, to the close of the age" (28:18-20). Or as it says in the longer ending of Mark's Gospel: "Go into all the world and preach the gospel to the whole creation. He who believes and is baptized will be saved; but he who does not believe will be condemned" (16:15-16). The Acts of the Apostles recounts that process of evangelical preaching and faithful response as it began in Jerusalem, where Peter concludes his Pentecost sermon thus: "Repent, and be baptized every one of you in the name of Jesus

Christ for the forgiveness of your sins; and you shall receive the gift of the Holy Spirit. For the promise is to you and to your children and to all that are far off, every one whom the Lord our God calls to him" (2:38-39). And "those who received his word were baptized, and there were added that day about three thousand souls" (2:41). Thus the Lima text is quite correct when it declares "baptism upon personal profession of faith is the most clearly attested pattern in the New Testament."[6] I may perhaps quietly reveal that it was I, as a member of the drafting group and editorial team for that WCC Faith and Order text, who made sure that that point was included.

What did the Lima text say more systematically about baptism? Baptism is "administered with water in the name of the Father, the Son and the Holy Spirit."[7] Its "meaning" was spelled out by *BEM* under five heads (we might rather call them its "benefits"): "Participation in Christ's Death and Resurrection"; "Conversion, Pardoning and Cleansing"; "The Gift of the Spirit"; "Incorporation into the Body of Christ"; and "The Sign of the Kingdom." Crucially for our present purposes, baptism was declared to be "both God's gift and our human response to that gift: it looks toward a growth into the measure of the stature of the fullness of Christ (Ephesians 4:13). The necessity of faith for the reception of the salvation embodied and set forth in baptism is acknowledged by all churches. Personal commitment is necessary for responsible membership in the body of Christ."[8]

Thus baptism entails both grace and faith. We might say that it is a focal point—or perhaps a decisive moment—in what is from God's side the process of grace, and what is from the human side the process of faith. God has been preparing the person for the gift of salvation, and now—in and through baptism—God administers "the seal of the Spirit" (long a traditional name for baptism). The recipient has been moving toward belief, and now professes it openly. Beyond baptism, God will continue to bestow grace to suit the condition and circumstances of the recipient, and the believer will expect to "grow in grace" through the exercise of faith in a loving direction after the pattern of Christ, into whose salvific death and resurrection he or she has been baptized with a view to the conquest of sin and the conduct and enjoyment of a qualitatively new and God-pleasing life.

The sixth chapter of St. Paul's Letter to the Romans gets us to the heart of the matter: "What shall we say then? Are we to continue in sin that grace may abound? By no means! How can we who died to sin still live in it? Do you not know that all of us who have been baptized into Christ Jesus were baptized into his death? We were buried therefore with him by baptism into death, so that as Christ was raised from the dead by the glory of the Father, we too might walk in newness of life." And so on.

My location of baptism within a process of grace and faith fits the responses of the churches to *BEM*, and it may help to settle the "dichotomy" between "infant baptism" and "believer baptism." I shall return to that matter under the ecumenical rubric of baptism and unity. Meanwhile I think I have done enough to show why St. Augustine could call baptism the "*sacramentum fidei*," the "sacrament of faith." Now we come explicitly to faith as a virtue, a divine gift that is to be exercised.

We have to speak of faith in two ways, which may be summarized in two related Latin phrases: the "*fides quae creditur*," and the "*fides quâ creditur*." That is, "the faith which is believed," and "the faith by which one believes." Or we can say "the content of the faith" and "the act of faith."

Let me illustrate from John Wesley's "Letter to a Roman Catholic," written from Dublin in July 1749 in an effort to allay Catholic opposition to the evangelistic work of the Methodists in Ireland. Wesley begins with the "tenderest regard" in which he must hold his addressee on account of their being creatures of the same God and their both being redeemed by God's own Son and "studying to have a conscience void of offence toward God and toward man." In the two main sections of the letter, Wesley then sets out "the belief of a true Protestant" and "the practice of a true Protestant," making the most of the commonalities between Protestants and Catholics. The *fides quae creditur*—the "content of the faith"—is presented in terms of an expansion upon the Nicene-Constantinopolitan Creed, bringing out the Chalcedonian teaching concerning the person and natures of Christ and the traditional understanding of Christ's "threefold office" as prophet, priest, and king. The *fides quâ creditur*—the "act or attitude of faith"—gets embodied in love toward God and neighbor, "works of piety" and "works of mercy." Together these constitute "the old religion," "true, primitive Christianity." And on that shared basis, Wesley says to his Catholic reader, "If we cannot as yet think alike in all things, at least we may love alike"; and so they should be kind to one another in thought, word, and deed, and finally "endeavour to help each other on in whatever we are agreed leads to the Kingdom": "So far as we can, let us always rejoice to strengthen each other's hands in God."[9]

Or again listen to how John Wesley in his sermon "On the Trinity"—without going into speculations on the internal structure of the Godhead—weaves together the *content* and the *act* of faith in respect of the Three-One God:

> The knowledge of the Three-One God is interwoven with all true Christian faith, with all vital religion. . . . I know not how anyone can be a Christian believer till "he hath" (as St. John speaks) "the witness in himself" [1 John 5:10]; till "the Spirit of God witnesses with his spirit that he is a child of God" [Romans 8:16]—that is, in effect, till God the Holy Ghost witnesses that God the Father has accepted him through the merits of God the Son—and having this witness he honours the Son and the blessed Spirit "even as he honours the Father" [John 5:23].[10]

In what shape or form is "faith" to be confessed, especially in crucial connection with baptism? Almost all churches in the West, whether Catholic or Protestant, employ the so-called Apostles' Creed in their baptismal rites; and the Orthodox churches of the East favor the Nicene-Constantinopolitan Creed. No opposition is to be seen between those two ancient and classical creeds. The point is to ensure that the faith being confessed in baptism is precisely the God-given faith of the Church, not simply an opinion of the person being baptized.

Steven Harmon—in a chapter written on Baptist tradition for a forthcoming *Oxford Handbook of Ecumenical Studies* of which I am an editor—reports that "when on July 5, 1905 the Baptist World Alliance met in London for its first congress, its newly elected president Alexander Maclaren invited participants to demonstrate Baptists' relation to the larger Christian tradition by reciting together the Apostles' Creed, 'not as a piece of coercion or discipline, but as a simple acknowledgment of where we stand and what we believe.'" Harmon elaborates: "The early Baptists received from the pre-Reformation church the canon of Scripture and the core doctrines of orthodox Christianity in light of which they read this canon. These gifts combined with their unique historical experiences as a socially embodied community to form a quintessentially Baptist pattern of faith and practice, at the core of which is ancient catholicity. Early Baptist confessions of faith underscored Baptist indebtedness to these gifts with language and concepts drawn directly from the ecumenical creeds, Anabaptist confessions, the Anglican Thirty-Nine Articles, and the Reformed Westminster Confession." Harmon instances two seventeenth-century Baptist confessions of faith in illustration of this Baptist reception of the creedal and confessional gifts of the rest of the church: the Second London Confession of the English Particular (Calvinistic) Baptists, 1677; and the Orthodox Creed of the English General (Arminian) Baptists, 1678. The latter reproduces the texts of the Apostles', Nicene, and Athanasian Creeds and encourages Baptists to receive and believe them. More recently, says Harmon, "Baptist hymnals have functioned as key facilitators of receptive ecumenism. They have helped Baptists to sing and receive the theologies of patristic and medieval Christianity, the Protestant Reformation, and a wide denominational variety of more recent hymn-writers including post-Reformation Catholics as well as Protestants of all stripes." The contemporary British Baptist Paul Fiddes suggests that Baptists might incorporate the broad contours of the catholic tradition into their worship through "the more regular use of the creeds" as acts of worship that "celebrate God's drama" and "present the Trinity as the supreme meta-narrative."[11]

I am aware that some Baptists hesitate—and even decline—to "recite" the creeds, lest the language or the conceptuality not be "their own," whereas faith must indeed be "personal." But let me give a counterexample from my own ecumenical experience: In the early 1980s, at the start of the

WCC Faith and Order Commission's "Apostolic Faith" study, there was considerable debate over the text to be taken as its basis. The Nicene-Constantinopolitan Creed was a contested proposal. A Jamaican Baptist, with perhaps confessional reservations in face of a text "imposed by imperial authority," and geographical or cultural doubts about the creed's "Greek metaphysics," was won over when he noticed that those who most *opposed* the use of the Nicene Creed were Western liberals, while its employment was advocated by other members of the Commission whose faith in the deity and redemptive work of Christ he shared. Thanks to Horace Russell, the Nicene Creed won the day to become the basis of *Confessing the One Faith*.[12]

Let me now return, as promised, to the matter of baptism, faith, and unity as it has presented itself since *Baptism, Eucharist and Ministry*. Notice first how paragraph 12 of "Baptism" makes the most of the similarities and common features between the two—"infant baptism" and "the baptism of believers":

Both the baptism of believers and the baptism of infants take place in the Church as the community of faith. When one who can answer for himself or herself is baptized, a personal confession of faith will be an integral part of the baptismal service. When an infant is baptized, the personal response will be offered at a later moment in life. In both cases, the baptized person will have to grow in the understanding of faith. For those baptized upon their own confession of faith,

17

there is always the constant requirement of a continuing growth of personal response in faith. In the case of infants, personal confession is expected later, and Christian nurture is directed to the eliciting of this confession. All baptism is rooted in and declares Christ's faithfulness unto death. It has its setting within the life and faith of the Church and, through the witness of the whole Church, points to the faithfulness of God, the ground of all life in faith. At every baptism the whole congregation reaffirms its faith in God and pledges itself to provide an environment of witness and service. Baptism should, therefore, always be celebrated and developed in the setting of the Christian community.

Within the initial document of *BEM*, the commentary to paragraph 12 goes on to hint that the two patterns—whether involving "infant baptism" or "believers' baptism"—might be viewed as "equivalent alternatives": "In some churches which unite both infant-baptist and believer-baptist traditions, it has been possible to regard as equivalent alternatives for entry into the Church both a pattern whereby baptism in infancy is followed by later profession of faith and a pattern whereby believers' baptism follows upon a presentation and blessing in infancy. This example invites other churches to decide whether they, too, could not recognize equivalent alternatives in their reciprocal relationships and church union negotiations."

Certainly the responses from the churches revealed "an increasing awareness that originally there was one complex rite of Christian initiation" and—in theological correspondence to that liturgico-historical observation—the churches were increasingly "coming to an understanding of initiation as a unitary and comprehensive process, even if its different elements are spread over a period of time," so that "the total process vividly embodies the coherence of God's gracious initiative in eliciting our faith." That is how Morris West, the British Baptist theologian, and I (a Methodist) were able to formulate the matter when, in our capacity as members of the WCC Faith and Order Commission, we were helping to draft the summary account of the churches' responses to *BEM*.[13]

On the ecumenical front, we must certainly notice over recent decades a clear tendency among the churches to what we may call "the mutual recognition of baptism." A hint—even if it remained in some ways unilateral—can already be found in the Second Vatican Council's "ecumenical decree," *Unitatis Redintegratio.* Concerning Christian brothers and sisters who are not members of the Roman Catholic Church, that decree declares, "Persons who believe in Christ and have been properly baptized are put in some measure of communion, albeit imperfect, with the Catholic Church [*in quadam cum Ecclesia catholica communione, etsi non perfecta, constituuntur*]." As to their communities:

> The brothers and sisters divided from us also carry
> out many liturgical actions of the Christian religion.

In ways that vary according to the condition of each Church or community, these liturgical actions most certainly can truly engender a life of grace, and, one must say, can aptly give access to the communion of salvation. It follows that the separated Churches and communities as such, though we believe they suffer from the defects already mentioned, have been by no means deprived of significance and importance in the mystery of salvation. For the Spirit of Christ has not refrained from using them as means of salvation which derive their efficacy from the very fullness of grace and truth entrusted to the Catholic Church (*UR*, 3).

What Protestants and their communities chiefly lack, according to the Roman Catholic view, is a succession in apostolic ministry—focused in the bishops in communion with the Bishop of Rome—with the authority to preach and teach the Christian faith infallibly.

Returning directly now to the mutual recognition of baptism, we find the following in paragraph 6 of *BEM*, where baptism is expounded as "incorporation into the Body of Christ": "Through baptism, Christians are brought into union with Christ, with each other, and with the Church of every time and place. Our common baptism, which unites us to Christ in faith, is thus a basic bond of unity. We are one people and are called to confess and serve one Lord in each place and in all the world." However, it was considered necessary to say in the commentary to that paragraph: "The inability of the churches mutually to recognize their various practices of baptism as sharing in the one baptism, and their actual dividedness in spite of mutual baptismal recognition, have given dramatic visibility to the broken witness of the Church. . . . The need to recover baptismal unity is at the heart of the ecumenical task as it is central for the realization of genuine partnership within the Christian communities."

The matter of the mutual recognition of baptism received attention at the Fifth World Conference on Faith and Order, held at Santiago de Compostela, Spain, in 1993. In particular, section 3 of the assembly made the following recommendations:

that Faith and Order put in process for consideration by the churches a way for the mutual recognition of each other's baptism by the churches;

that, where this is possible but not already done, the churches develop a common baptismal certificate;

that churches invite neighbour churches to participate in baptism in appropriate ways.

Baptism has, in fact, figured quite prominently among the topics treated by the Faith and Order Commission since then. Evidence is found in Thomas F. Best's edited volume *Baptism Today*, where the current understandings and practices are reported.[14] The complex challenges addressed to the churches then figure in the Faith and Order "study text" *One Baptism*.[15] Highly significant is the study already contained in the Joint

Working Group's "Ecclesiological and Ecumenical Implications of a Common Baptism."[16] Especially in connection with divergences over infant baptism—but the areas of dispute are wider—the report recognizes among the issues needing resolution "the questions of the nature and purposes of the Church and its role in the economy of salvation" (para. 57); and notes soberly that "the mutual recognition of baptism implies an acknowledgment of each other's baptism, but in itself is only a step toward full recognition of the apostolicity of the church involved" (para. 98). The question must be put in any constellation of presently divided "churches" among which mutual recognition of baptism exists: What more do you require of the partners—and of yourself—before you can discern "church"?

Up to now I have been thinking chiefly of "our" faith—faith as a gift from God to "us." But we, as Christians, are not meant to keep this faith "to ourselves." It is a gift to be propagated. Listen to this passage from Paul's Second Letter to the Corinthians (4:13-15), where the apostle compares himself and his fellow evangelist Timothy to the psalmist of Psalm 116:10: "Since we have the same spirit of faith as he had who wrote 'I believed, and so I spoke,' we too believe, and so we speak, knowing that he who raised the Lord Jesus will raise us also with Jesus and bring us with you into his presence. For it is all for your sake, so that as grace extends to more and more people it may increase thanksgiving, to the glory of God." Faith is meant to be spoken out, to be rendered in testimony to the gospel, so that more and more people may become believers and become incorporated into the eucharistic community—about which I will be saying more when we arrive at the Lord's Supper.

Meanwhile I simply note that the modern "ecumenical movement" is generally reckoned to date from the World Missionary Conference of Edinburgh 1910. The International Missionary Council was founded in 1921 and became integrated with the World Council of Churches in 1961. From "Edinburgh 1910" sprang, moreover, not only "mission and evangelism" but also, as a needed consequence, the "faith and order" stream of ecumenism. Common witness risks disruption if there is division in matters of doctrine or ecclesial structure—which may indeed be a countertestimony to the gospel. That "faith and order" as well as "mission and evangelism" belong at the heart of classical ecumenism may be seen in exemplary fashion from the case of the Church of South India. Formed in 1947 from the organic union of the fruits of missionary labors in the subcontinent, the Church of South India rested on an agreed basis of doctrine and worship, unified structures of ministry and government, and commitment to a vigorously envisaged continuation of indigenous evangelism.

With that prospect we make our transition from "faith" to "hope."

HOPE AND THE LORD'S PRAYER
࿇

For the move from faith to hope we may find help in the first verse of the Letter to the Hebrews, chapter 11: "Now faith is the *substance* of things hoped for, the *evidence* of things not seen" (KJV); "Now faith is the *assurance* of things hoped for, the *conviction* of things not seen" (RSV). The chapter goes on to give historic examples of various kinds. The Greek words *hupostasis* and *elegchos* are quite technical terms, with a range of philosophical associations. We might say that the CONTENT of faith is what "grounds" or "underlies" hope; it is what things hoped for "stand upon." And the ACT of faith gives "insight" into things "not (yet) seen." Considering hope as a "theological virtue," we may emphasize not only its future direction but its eschatological range; and it will find its liturgical match in the Lord's Prayer. Raymond Brown, noted Catholic New

Testament scholar of the mid-to-late twentieth century, wrote a thirty-five-page exegesis of the Our Father precisely under the title "The Pater Noster as an Eschatological Prayer." Ray Brown was my closest friend and colleague during my short time of teaching at Union Theological Seminary in New York and during the earliest years of my membership in the international dialogue between the World Methodist Council and the Roman Catholic Church; and I draw with confidence upon his work.[17]

A solid and prominent theme of New Testament scholarship in the twentieth century was the kingdom of God—with, of course, nuances among the exegetes as to its understanding. Unquestioned was the connection between the kingdom of God and Jesus—as to his person, his preaching and teaching (think of C. H. Dodd's classic *The Parables of the Kingdom*), his social activity and mighty deeds, his death and resurrection, and indeed his expected return. Scholars varied only as to the temporal stages of the kingdom's coming in its multiform association with Jesus and as to possible shifts in its timing and interpretation as the oral and written witness of the New Testament authors evolved.

Let me jump boldly into the Lord's Prayer and—off my own bat—take "Thy kingdom come" as its key petition around which the other clauses cluster. As to the second in our trio of virtues—that of hope—we may say that in and through the Prayer taught by the Lord Jesus, believers are given a confident hope to enjoy and exercise in the direction of God's final kingdom—all the way along to its final achievement.

In the very address—"Our Father, who art in heaven"—Jesus associates his disciples with himself in access to the prime and ultimate Ruler of all. Says Raymond Brown,

> In the New Testament, God's Fatherhood is . . . put on the basis of union with Jesus, who is God's Son in a special way. He alone can call God "my Father" in the proper sense; those who unite themselves to Him share His power to do so through God's gift. This New Testament concept of God's Fatherhood and Christian sonship gives an eschatological tone to the title of the Pater Noster, for if we examine the Synoptic Gospels carefully, we find that becoming sons of God is something that happens in the last days and in the heavenly kingdom [cf. Matthew 5:9; 13:38, 43; Luke 6:35; 20:36]. . . . Hence, if in the Pater Noster Christians can address God as "Father," it is because they are anticipating their state of perfection, which will come at the close of this age. They are anticipating the coming of God's eschatological kingdom, which is already incipient in the preaching of Jesus."[18]

Other New Testament writings may phrase things differently, says Brown, but there is no contradiction:

> Paul and John treat sonship as a gift already conferred (in Paul's thought, by adoption [Galatians 4:5];

in John's thought, by divine begetting [John 1:12-13; 3:5; 1 John 3:9; also 1 Peter 1:23]). This is an aspect of "realized eschatology." We believe that both views of divine sonship stem from the mind of Christ. . . . Both views are true: we are God's sons now through sanctifying grace; but this sonship will be perfected in ultimate union with God. And both Paul and John recognized this: cf. Romans 8:23: "We ourselves who have the first fruits of the Spirit groan inwardly as we wait for adoption as sons, the redemption of our bodies"; 1 John 3:2: "We are God's children now; it does not yet appear what we shall be; but we know that when he appears, we shall be like him."[19]

Now to the interpretation of the several petitions of the Lord's Prayer, with an eye to the match with the virtue of hope. We shall, where appropriate, shade our interpretations to the stage in which we now find ourselves in relation to God's kingdom—between the first coming of Christ and his final coming. The way to God's final kingdom may be gradual but not necessarily even. In view of the barriers of sin, failure, corruption, and death, Lesslie Newbigin would say in his Bangalore Lectures of 1941 that there is no straight line of development from here to the kingdom. In this context, hope must come into play.[20]

If we think in terms of the classic streams of ecumenism in the twentieth century, it is perhaps in relation to "life and work" that hope first comes on the scene: in this "time between the times," Christians and their communities may cooperate in promoting the values of God's kingdom in the civic and social areas of existence. However, the eschatological horizon must not be forgotten, whether for each person and family, or for the ecclesial and secular communities, or for humankind in its entirety. There are ultimate matters of vocation and destiny for all. The Westminster Catechism famously asks, "What is the chief end of man? Man's chief end is to glorify God, and to enjoy Him for ever."

Now again to the Lord's Prayer, and we begin this time with the first petition: "Hallowed be thy name." The linguists sometimes tell us that the passive voice is a Semitic idiom indicating that only God, who alone in himself is holy, can make manifest the sanctity of his own name. A similar argument might perhaps be made in the case of the third petition: "Thy will be done on earth as it is in heaven." For my part, I would not wish to exclude at least a secondarily active role for God's creatures in these respects—in the acknowledgment of God's holiness as well as in cooperation toward the full and final achievement of God's will as the universal manifestation of his glory. That would include us humans who were and are "made in the image of God" with a view to "attaining his likeness" (Genesis 1:26-27). A variant reading in Luke's version of the Lord's Prayer phrases the second petition as "May your Holy Spirit come upon us and purify us." When, in Acts 1:6-8,

29

the disciples ask about the coming of God's kingdom, Jesus answers them in terms of the coming of the Holy Spirit.

The tone may appear to shift in the fourth petition of the Lord's Prayer: "Give us this day our daily bread." But even such a modest request would not be unsuitable to God's patient provision for us along the historical way to the final kingdom. The petition may become more exciting if we look more closely at the strange word *epiousios*. The linguistics are complicated, but what we are perhaps being instructed to pray for is "our tomorrow's bread," where the eschatological resonance would not be far to seek: Christians are then praying for the bread that will be given at the heavenly table, where the saints will hunger no more but rather feast openly with Christ (cf. Luke 6:21; 14:15; and esp. 22:29-30). In my early book *Eucharist and Eschatology*, I traced how the historic liturgies of the Church echo and develop the Gospel sayings concerning the "sacramental" feeding on Christ as the Bread from heaven, the Bread of life, in prayerful and hopeful anticipation of the heavenly banquet in the final kingdom.[21]

But meanwhile the Lord's Prayer brings us back to earth in the fifth petition: "Forgive us our trespasses, as we forgive those who trespass against us." Along the way, we are encouraged to mutual forgiveness and reconciliation, as various Gospel sayings and parables make clear. Raymond Brown summarizes:

> In the last days the followers of Christ will receive the fullness of divine sonship. Their forgiveness of one

30

another as brothers and sisters and their forgiveness by their Father are both parts of this great gift. In the fifth petition of the Pater Noster they stand by anticipation before the throne of God; and they request the supreme and final act of fatherly forgiveness, even as they extend the complete and final act of brotherly forgiveness. This forgiveness in both directions removes all obstacles to the perfect community of the heavenly banquet table for which they have asked in the fourth petition.[22]

In the sixth petition, Christians are praying for "preservation from the final diabolic onslaught" or deliverance from the "titanic struggle with Satan that stands between the community and the realization of its prayer." "The return of Christ," says Raymond Brown, "comes persistently closer each day"; and the scholar concludes his eschatological exegesis of the Lord's Prayer by remarking that "the Pater Noster, said as a fervent *maranatha*, would not be an inappropriate welcome."[23]

In establishing the match between the virtue of faith and the dominically instituted rite of holy baptism, we looked for support in the sixth chapter of the Letter to the Romans. In showing now the match between the virtue of hope and the pattern of the Lord's own prayer, we may turn to the eighth chapter of that Pauline Epistle. Declaring to "those who are in Christ Jesus" (v. 1) that "you are in the Spirit, if in fact the Spirit of God dwells in you" (v. 9), the apostle promises that "if the Spirit of him who raised Christ Jesus from the dead dwells in you, he who raised Christ Jesus from the dead will give life to your mortal bodies also through his Spirit which dwells in you" (v. 11). And "we ourselves, who have the first fruits of the Spirit, groan inwardly as we wait for adoption as sons, the redemption of our bodies. For in this hope we were saved. Now hope that is seen is not hope. For who hopes for what he sees? But if we hope for what we do not see, we wait for it with patience" (vv. 23-25). And all this is set in the context of prayer, which Christians as God's adopted children are privileged to say in terms of "Abba, Father" (vv. 12-17). And when "in our weakness, we do not know how to pray as we ought, the Spirit himself intercedes for us, according to the will of God" (vv. 26-27). The apostle goes on to say that "in everything God works for good with those who love him, who are called according to his purpose" (v. 28), and he voices the assurance that neither now nor in the final testing will anything be able to "separate us from the love of God in Christ Jesus our Lord" (vv. 31-39). Such is the present and ultimate match between hope and prayer according to Christ.

Thus guided by Romans 8, the praying of the Lord's Prayer may perhaps be characterized as "hope in action"—an instance of the cooperation of humans with God for the sake finally of God's glory and their salvation.

What now are the ecumenical dimensions of this combination of hope and the dominical prayer with a view more precisely to unity among Christians and between their various communities?

Let me begin anecdotally. I well remember from my days as an undergraduate at the University of Cambridge in the late 1950s that—from the Roman Catholic side—the only religious act that was permissible between Catholics and Protestants was the saying of the Lord's Prayer together. From the Catholic side, that was only a recently accorded permission. For many of us—on both sides—those occasions were special moments of grace.

In the earliest centuries of our era, the Lord's Prayer was delivered and taught to all new Christians in connection with their baptism.[24] A patristic text which highlights the themes of salvific hope and Christian unity in its exposition of the Our Father is the treatise on the Lord's Prayer from the hand of St. Cyprian of Carthage in the mid-third century, which we may now follow.[25] The Gospel precepts, which include the Lord's Prayer, "are nothing else than divine teachings—foundations on which to build hope, supports to strengthen faith, foods to nourish the heart, guides to direct our journey, guards on the way to salvation—which, while they instruct the receptive minds of believers on the earth, lead them to the heavenly realms." As to "*our* Father," he is "the Father of those who believe—of those who, being sanctified by him, and restored by the birth of spiritual grace, have begun to be children of God." And "when we call God Father, we ought to act as

God's children." By praying for the divine will to be done by those who are still "on earth"—that is, those who do not yet believe—believers are by divine instruction meantime "praying for the salvation of all." Gathered for prayer, Christians do not say "Give me this day my daily bread"; rather, "our prayer is common and collective; and when we pray, we pray not for one, but for the whole people, because we are all one people together." "The God of peace and the Teacher of concord, who taught unity, willed that one should thus pray for all, just as he himself bore the weight of all of us together." Invoking Matthew 5:23-24 on the need for reconciliation before the making of an offering, Cyprian writes, "Our peace and fraternal agreement is the greater sacrifice to God—and a people united in the unity of the Father, and of the Son, and of the Holy Spirit." Invoking Acts 1:14 for the sake of the apostles and the women with Mary the mother of Jesus, who after the Lord's ascension "continued with one accord in prayer," Cyprian concludes that God "admits into the divine and eternal home only those who are of one mind in prayer."

Arriving in chapter 30 of his treatise at John 17, Cyprian came to the Lord's words that have been such an inspiration to those committed to the ecumenical cause of restored unity among divided Christians: the Lord Jesus envisages more than his immediate apostles when, on the eve of his suffering, he "entreats the Father for all" with the words "Neither do I pray for these alone, but for those also who shall believe in me through their word, that they all may be one, as thou, Father, art in me, and I in thee, that they also may be in us." Cyprian continues:

> Great alike is the Lord's kindness, no less than his mercy, in respect of our salvation, in that, not content to redeem us with his blood, he in addition also prayed for us. And see now what was the desire of his petition, that just as the Father and the Son are one, so also we should abide in that unity. From this it may be understood how greatly one sins who rends unity and peace. That is why the Lord prayed thus for his people, wishing that they should have life, since he knew that discord cannot enter into the kingdom of God.

There is also another evangelical text which paints a cameo or an icon of Christians joining together to pray—under dominical inspiration—for the unity of the Church. According to Matthew 18:19-20, Jesus encouraged his disciples in this way: "Again I say to you, if two of you agree on earth about anything they ask, it will be done for them by my Father in heaven. For where two or three are gathered in my name, there am I in the midst of them." Hearing the Lord speak those words, one can almost catch a glimpse of the representatives from the WCC Faith and Order Commission and the Pontifical Council for Promoting Christian Unity gathered in their annual meeting in order to settle on the themes and texts for next year's Week of Prayer for Christian Unity. And let it finally be mentioned that the vision of the ecumenical partners will extend to the end of the sentence in John 17:21: "That they all may be one—even as thou, Father, art in me, and I in thee, that they also may be one in us, so that the world may believe that thou hast sent me." "*Ut unum sint, . . . ut mundus credat*": unity among Christians and their communities is integral to Christians' missionary witness and thus to the hope for the world's coming to faith in the Lord, and thereby to salvation.

Let me mention one more ecumenical feature which, in a matching of hope and prayer, may bring the final kingdom of God qualitatively—if not temporally—nearer. When I first became a member of the WCC Faith and Order Commission, its "Study of Hope" was being concluded; and at the plenary meeting in Bangalore, India, in 1978, I was asked to chair the drafting group that would prepare a sectional report on martyrdom as "ultimate hope" that would figure—under the heading "Witness Unto Death"—as the final section of the main document. Here is the thrust of what we said:

> In the witness of the martyrs we may rediscover the effective work of Christ who breaks down the barriers erected by sin and human weakness. In the martyrs the Church discerns Christ himself, beyond all interpretations and divisions. That is why the martyrs of the early Church and some great witnesses in the later history of the Church are the common property of all Christians. . . . The martyr bears witness to the living God and to the coming of his kingdom. By his death

he contests all attitudes which would absolutize the present state of affairs. Yet Christian hope does not demobilize us with regard to engagement in history. On the contrary, it supplies reasons for such involvement and the courage to undertake it. The Christian knows that he or she is sharing in the work of God which aims to bring about a new creation. Hope inspires acts or attitudes which announce the definitive kingdom of God.[26]

Already the Second Vatican Council, in acknowledging "the truly Christian endowments for our common heritage which are to be found among our separated brethren," had mentioned in particular "the riches of Christ and virtuous works in the lives of others who are bearing witness to Christ, sometimes even to the shedding of their blood."[27] Pope John Paul II, in his 1995 encyclical *Ut Unum Sint*, developed the thought that all Christian communities "have martyrs for the Christian faith": "We Christians already have a common martyrology." Full communion extends to all the saints, "those who, at the end of a life faithful to grace, are in communion with Christ in glory": "These Saints come from all the Churches and Ecclesial Communities which gave them entrance into the communion of salvation. When we speak of a common heritage, we must acknowledge as part of that not only the institutions, rites, means of salvation, and the traditions which all the communities have preserved and by which they have been shaped, but first and foremost this reality of holiness."[28] Our common martyrology—and indeed the heavenly "communion of all the saints"—entails, we may say, a fellowship also for us in prayer.

A suitable liturgical ending for this second lecture would be precisely the prayer for All Saints' Day in the classic *Book of Common Prayer*, where the virtues of hope and love are implicitly combined and thus help prepare for our third lecture, "Love and the Lord's Supper." The collect runs: "O almighty God, who hast knit together thine elect in one communion and fellowship, in the mystical body of the Son Christ our Lord: Grant us grace so to follow thy blessed Saints in all virtuous and godly living, that we may come to those unspeakable joys, which thou hast prepared for them that unfeignedly love thee, through Jesus Christ our Lord. Amen." Or with Charles Wesley:

Come, let us join our friends above
That have obtained the prize,
And on the eagle wings of love
To joys celestial rise:
Let all the saints terrestrial sing
With those to glory gone;
For all the servants of our King
In earth and heaven are one.[29]

Up to now in the lectures we have, in fact, considered the first two in our "ecumenical trio of virtues": faith and hope. Each has been matched with an institution of the Lord's: faith with holy baptism, and hope with the Lord's Prayer. The content and the act of Christian faith find expression and exercise in the rite of trinitarian baptism ordained by the risen Christ. The substance and the direction of hope are sketched and guided by the eschatological Pater Noster and other prayers of Jesus, all said in the Holy Spirit. Returning to the last verse of the thirteenth chapter in Paul's First Letter to the Corinthians, we find that there "now abideth faith, hope, charity, these three; but the greatest of these is charity." We come finally, then, to our third virtue—that of love, where the match is to be made with the Lord's Supper.

LOVE AND THE LORD'S SUPPER
ℬ

According to the Fourth Gospel, we find that "when Jesus knew that his hour had come to depart out of the world and go to the Father, having loved his own who were in the world, he loved them to the end" (John 13:1). At the Last Supper as reported in the Third Gospel we find Jesus saying to his disciples, "I am among you as one who serves. You are those who have continued with me in my trials; and I assign to you, as my Father assigned to me, a kingdom, that you may eat and drink at my table in my kingdom" (Luke 22:28-29). The three Synoptic Gospels and Paul all record how Jesus on that final occasion bequeathed what would become known as the Lord's Supper or even, as by the Second Vatican Council, the "*sacramentum caritatis*," the "sacrament of love."[30]

Here is the account of the apostle Paul in his First Epistle to the Corinthians:

> I received from the Lord what I also delivered to you, that the Lord Jesus on the night when he was betrayed took bread, and when he had given thanks, he broke it, and said, "This is my body which is broken for you. Do this in remembrance of me." In the same way also the cup, after supper, saying, "This cup is the new covenant in my blood. Do this, as often as you drink it, in remembrance of me." For as often as you eat this bread and drink the cup, you proclaim the Lord's death until he comes (1 Corinthians 11:23-26).

The Lord's Supper is the rite in which the love of the Lord Jesus is demonstrated and experienced, whereby the virtue of love may be inculcated among the immediate recipients and even extended beyond them through their corresponding conduct.

On this occasion we cannot trace the entire liturgical history of the Eucharist, but I would like to begin by recalling the service with which I grew up in the Methodist Church of Great Britain. The first order for "The Lord's Supper, or The Holy Communion" in our 1936 *Book of Offices* followed quite closely "The Order for the Administration of the Lord's Supper, or Holy Communion" in the 1662 *Book of Common Prayer* of the Church of England. Let me quote from our Methodist book; and I ask you to notice the frequency and range of the "love" that there comes to expression.[31]

After the initial "Our Father" the opening "collect" ran thus: "Almighty God, unto whom all hearts be open, all desires known, and from whom no secrets are hid: Cleanse the thoughts of our hearts by the inspiration of Thy Holy Spirit, that we may perfectly LOVE Thee and worthily magnify Thy holy Name; through Christ our Lord. Amen."

The rubric follows: "Then shall the Minister rise, and, turning to the People, rehearse distinctly the Commandments of the Lord Jesus; and the People still kneeling shall, after every commandment, ask of God mercy for their transgression thereof for the time past, and grace to keep the same for time to come, as follows:

Our Lord Jesus Christ said: The first commandment is, Hear, O Israel, the Lord our God, the Lord is one; and thou shalt LOVE the Lord thy God with all thy heart, and with all thy soul, and with all thy mind, and with all thy strength.

Lord, have mercy upon us, and incline our hearts to keep this law.

The second is this: Thou shalt LOVE thy neighbour as thyself. There is none other commandment greater than these.

Lord, have mercy upon us, and incline our hearts to keep this law.

A new commandment I give unto you, That ye LOVE one another; even as I have LOVED you, that ye also LOVE one another.

Lord, have mercy upon us, and write these Thy laws in our heart, we beseech Thee."

After the Scripture readings (Epistle and Gospel) comes the prayer "For the whole estate of Christ's Church militant here on earth," where we are reminded that we are "to make prayers and supplications, and to give thanks for all men," and pray God to "inspire continually the universal Church with the spirit of truth, unity, and concord," asking God to grant that "all they that do confess Thy holy Name, may agree in the truth of Thy holy word, and live in unity and GODLY LOVE."

Then comes the minister's exhortation to intending communicants, who are supposed to "be in PERFECT CHARITY with all men," if they are properly to receive what Christ "instituted and ordained" as "PLEDGES OF HIS LOVE": "Ye therefore that do truly and earnestly repent of your sins, and are in LOVE and CHARITY with your neighbours. . . . Draw near with faith, and take this holy Sacrament to your comfort." Then, in immediate preparation for communion, come the "comfortable words our Saviour Christ saith unto all that truly turn to Him," on which all our faith, hope, and love are founded, inevitably including these: "God so LOVED the world, that He gave His only begotten Son, that whosoever believeth on Him should not perish, but have eternal life."

After all that wordage, let us look now also at some gestures and some dispositions of space that embody the divine and human love enacted in the *sacramentum caritatis*, drawing a little more widely on liturgical history and practice.

A first gesture may go back to St. Paul when he urged the Roman Christians to "greet one another with a holy kiss" (Romans 16:15). I am thinking, however, of the exchange of "the peace" that has spread rapidly among many Protestant churches by way of the influential liturgy of the Church of South India, which had brought into union in 1947 the fruits of missionary labors especially on the part of British Anglicans, Methodists, Presbyterians, and Congregationalists in that region of the subcontinent. The form of the gesture combined one used by Orthodox Christians there with the hand motion and bow common in Indian society. Not that the gesture became immediately accepted by all Christians in the home countries. My own mother used to say that she "came to church to worship God, not to shake hands with Mrs. So-and-So"; and she would certainly not have welcomed the development of "the peace" into the "hugging and kissing" now present in many Methodist services.

Other, perhaps less controversial, gestures favored by the "liturgical movement" included the presentation of foodstuffs and other items at the offertory, which were then distributed to the needy after the service; or again, the use of a single loaf and a single cup for the Holy Communion, with the delivery of consecrated remains for the prolongation of the sacramental service among housebound members of the congregation.

If, as I did for the match between faith and baptism and that between hope and the "Abba" prayer, I were to look into the Letter to the Romans for a match between love and the Lord's Supper, I could turn to the fifteenth chapter, where the apostle rounds on the disputatious characters from chapter fourteen: "May the God of steadfastness [*hupomonē*] and encouragement [*paraklēsis*]"—those are qualities and gifts associated with the Holy Spirit—"grant you to be of one mind [*to auto phronein*] among yourselves, that you may with one heart or will [*homothumadon*] and one mouth or voice [*en heni stomati*] glorify the God and Father of our Lord Jesus Christ" (15:5-6). If, after all that, Paul charged the Romans to "welcome one another, as Christ has welcomed you, for the glory of God" (15:7) and then prayed that "the God of hope fill you with all joy and peace in believing, so that by the power of the Holy Spirit you may abound in hope" (15:13), then it will scarcely be stretching matters to say that, according to the apostle, not only unity in faith and unity in hope but also unity in love belong to proper participation in the high prayers of the Eucharist and in the bread and wine of the Lord's Supper, sealed perhaps with a holy kiss (16:16); and such indeed he hammers home to the fractious Corinthians in his first letter to the church in Corinth (especially in chapters 1, 10, and 11).

In Christian history, the Lord's Supper—ironically—has often been the scene where disputes and divisions have arisen or been maintained. These disturbances have concerned both matters of doctrine and matters of discipline. In connection with the Lord's Supper itself, the doctrinal matters have mainly touched on the nature and mode of Christ's presence at the Supper, and on the relation between the eucharistic action and the unique sacrifice of Christ; the disciplinary matters have had to do with authority to preside at the Lord's Table and with competence to receive the sacramental bread and wine in communion. Such issues of doctrine and discipline have also been labeled questions of "faith" and "order," and the chief forum for attempting their ecumenical settlement in our time has been the Faith and Order Commission of the World Council of Churches.

The most remarkable evidence in that connection was the "convergence text," *Baptism, Eucharist and Ministry (BEM)*, which was unanimously adopted by the Plenary Commission of Faith and Order at Lima, Peru, in January 1982 as "mature" for transmission to the churches with the request for evaluation, including "the extent to which your church can recognize in this text the faith of the Church through the ages; the consequences your church can draw from this text for its relations and dialogues with other churches, particularly with those churches which also recognize the text as an expression of the apostolic faith; the guidance your church can take from this text for its worship, educational, ethical, and spiritual life and witness." The text attracted an unprecedented amount of attention among ecumenically engaged denominations and their membership.

With regard to the Eucharist, it is generally agreed that there must be at least a reasonable measure of agreement as to what is taking place around the Lord's Table before ecclesial communion can be shared—and finally restored—among hitherto divided communities claiming to be "church." It was therefore gratifying that the most concise paragraph on "The Meaning of the Eucharist" found a practically unanimous welcome:

> The eucharist is essentially the sacrament of the gift which God makes to us in Christ through the power of the Holy Spirit. Every Christian receives salvation through communion in the body and blood of Christ. In the eucharistic meal, in the eating and drinking of the bread and wine, Christ grants communion with himself. God himself acts, giving life to the body of Christ and renewing each member. In accordance with Christ's promise, each baptized member of the body of Christ receives in the eucharist the assurance of the forgiveness of sins (Matt. 26:28) and the pledge of eternal life (John 6:51-58). [32]

Again the respondents delighted in a sentence from paragraph 13 ("The Church confesses Christ's real, living and active presence in the eucharist"), but already an original commentary on that paragraph had signaled a warning that the churches differed as to how definite was the link between the presence of Christ and "the signs of bread and wine." To the question of "whether this difference can be accommodated within the convergence formulated in the [full] text itself [of paragraph 13]," the replies—sometimes from opposite directions—came in negatively.

As to the relation between the eucharistic action and Christ's unique sacrifice, paragraph 5 exploited the redis-covered biblical notion of "anamnesis" or "memorial": "The eucharist is the memorial of the crucified and risen Christ, i.e. the living and effective sign of his sacrifice accomplished once and for all on the cross and still operative on behalf of all humankind. The biblical idea of memorial as applied to the eucharist refers to this present efficacy of God's work when it is celebrated by God's people in a liturgy." Paragraph 8 contin-ues: "The eucharist is the sacrament of the unique sacrifice of Christ, who ever lives to make intercession for us. . . . In the memorial of the eucharist, the Church offers its intercession in communion with Christ, our great High Priest."

As to the presidency at the Lord's Table, paragraph 29 declares: "In the celebration of the eucharist, Christ gathers, teaches and nourishes the Church. It is Christ who invites to the meal and who presides at it. He is the shepherd who leads the people of God, the prophet who announces the Word of God, the priest who celebrates the mystery of God. In most churches, this presidency is signified by an ordained minis-ter."[33] As to churches which lack a putatively uninterrupted succession of apostolic ministry, the idea was floated in para-graph 38 of *BEM*'s "Ministry" section that they might come to appreciate (and then presumably receive) "the episcopal succession as a sign, though not a guarantee, of the continuity and unity of the Church," but the replies from the various churches revealed that the idea of "a sign, though not a guarantee" was too much for some and too little for others.

Reverting directly to the *BEM* text on the Eucharist, we find in paragraph 19 the following affirmations concerning "The Eucharist as Communion of the Faithful":

> The eucharistic communion with Christ who nourishes the life of the Church is at the same time communion within the body of Christ which is the Church. The sharing in one bread and the common cup in a given place demonstrates and effects the oneness of the sharers with Christ and with their fellow sharers in all times and places. It is in the eucharist that the community of God's people is fully manifested. Eucharistic celebrations always have to do with the whole Church, and the whole Church is involved in each local eucharistic celebration. In so far as a church claims to be a manifestation of the whole Church, it will take care to order its own life in ways which take seriously the interests and concerns of other churches.

What, then, are we to make of the *lack* of communion between "churches"?

The final chapter on "The Celebration of the Eucharist" (paras. 27–33) makes several proposals to help bring eucharistic communion closer to its proper role in ecclesial communion. Thus:

28. The best way toward unity in eucharistic celebration and communion is the renewal of the eucharist itself in the different churches in regard to teaching and liturgy. The churches should test their liturgies in the light of the eucharistic agreement now in process of attainment. The liturgical reform movement has brought the churches closer together in the manner of celebrating the Lord's Supper. However, a certain liturgical diversity compatible with our common eucharistic faith is recognized as a healthy and enriching fact. . . .

30. Christian faith is deepened by the celebration of the Lord's Supper. Hence the eucharist should be celebrated frequently. Many differences of theology, liturgy and practice are connected with the varying frequency with which the Holy Communion is celebrated.

31. As the eucharist celebrates the resurrection of Christ, it is appropriate that it should take place at least every Sunday. As it is the new sacramental meal of the people of God, every Christian should be encouraged to receive communion frequently. . . .

33. The increased mutual understanding expressed in the present statement may allow some churches to

attain a greater measure of eucharistic communion among themselves and so bring closer the day when Christ's divided people will be visibly reunited around the Lord's Table.

With that, we come to our last current question concerning the Lord's Supper as "the sacrament of love"; it is a question that has occupied ecumenists since the start of the modern ecumenical movement, namely that of "eucharistic sharing." At what stage along the way to the restoration of unity among divided churches does it become proper to share communion across confessional or denominational lines? The question has usually revolved around the term "intercommunion."[34]

For much of the twentieth century, "intercommunion" was the slogan around which the ecumenical debate turned regarding the point at which churches might properly enter into eucharistic fellowship with one another. The Orthodox rejected altogether the notion of *inter*communion—name and thing—on the ground that there is either "communion" in the one Church or no communion at all. A similar substantive position was held by the Roman Catholic Church, some Anglicans, some Lutherans, and some Baptists, although these all differed on what was required for the unity of which eucharistic communion was or would be the sacramental expression. On the other hand, those churches which accepted a "federal" model of unity used the word "intercommunion" without any pejorative intent or sense of provisionality, to describe their sacramental sharing across persisting denominational boundaries.

Between those two positions stood those ecumenists who had most at stake in the notion of intercommunion. At some point along the road to an ever-fuller unity, they argued, it becomes appropriate—both possible and desirable—for churches to practice intercommunion as both a sign of the measure of unity they already enjoy and a means toward a more perfect unity. Sometimes adopting an eschatological perspective (for the Lord's Supper prefigures the banquet of the final kingdom, where a divided fellowship is unthinkable), they argued that the goal of unity could become proleptically effective through the active anticipation of it in the sacrament. At the time of the Faith and Order Conference in Lund in 1952, T. F. Torrance spoke of the Eucharist as "the divinely given Sacrament of unity, indeed the medicine for our divisions."[35]

Now as to liturgical practice, especially at meetings in the multilateral versions of the ecumenical movement: in the heyday of the World Council of Churches, the practice became established—formalized by the Central Committee in 1963 upon recommendation from the World Conference on Faith and Order at Montreal in that year—of including on the official program of big ecumenical conferences both a Eucharist "according to the liturgy of a church which cannot conscientiously offer an invitation to members of all other churches to partake of the elements" and one "in which a church or group of churches can invite members of other churches to participate and partake." This dual practice witnessed to disagreements among the churches about whether eucharistic communion was a means on the road to unity or rather the goal of the journey; and more will be said about that in a moment. In the ecumenical case, "occasional communion" was not understood on an individualistic basis, as though participants took part as "private persons." Rather, all who figured in the celebration, in whatever liturgical role, acted and received communion in some sense as representatives of the churches or ecclesial communities to which they belonged.

The dual pattern was abandoned at the Eighth Assembly of the WCC, held at Harare (Zimbabwe) in 1998. At the previous instigation of the Orthodox, there was to be no Eucharist in the general program of the meeting, but rather a vigil of "confession and repentance for our brokenness," of penitence for the inability to eat together at the Lord's Table.

From the larger ecclesiastical scene may we narrow our question to that of "eucharistic hospitality" as it has come to be known and practiced in the area of individual pastoral care? We may first take an example from what has traditionally been the stricter side, namely the Roman Catholic. The Second Vatican Council offered hospitality, in exceptional circumstances, to Orthodox Christians in the sacraments of penance, Eucharist, and the anointing of the sick.[36] Protestants have been included in the provisions made in the Ecumenical Directories of 1967

(no. 55) and 1993 (nos. 129–31)—and endorsed by Pope John
Paul II both in the 1995 encyclical *Ut Unum Sint* (no. 46) and in
the 2003 encyclical *Ecclesia de Eucharistia* (no. 46)—for rightly
disposed non-Catholics to receive, upon request, the Catholic
Eucharist in the emergency circumstances of mortal danger,
persecution, imprisonment, or serious spiritual need. A condition is that the sacramental faith of such seekers be consonant
with the Catholic faith. That pastoral opening may have hitherto unexplored implications for the way in which the Catholic Church might view the sacramental and ecclesial reality of
Protestant bodies, for where else would such communicants
have come to their faith except in their own communities? In
the other direction, the latter encyclical repeats the injunction
that "Catholics may not receive communion in those communities which lack a valid sacrament of Orders" (no. 46; cf. no. 30).
In the same context, Pope John Paul repeats the prohibition
against any Catholic involvement in "concelebration" or "intercommunion" before "the visible bonds of ecclesial communion
are fully re-established" (nos. 44–45). Such actions, he warns,
"might well prove instead to be *an obstacle to the attainment of full
communion*, by weakening the sense of how far we remain from
this goal and by introducing or exacerbating ambiguities with
regard to one or another truth of the faith. The path toward full
unity can only be undertaken in truth" (emphasis in original).

Undoubtedly the Pope's warning against any premature
mutuality of eucharistic communion, or any acquiescence in

inadequate forms of unity, is both authoritative for Catholics and salutary for the broader ecumenical movement. Yet when John Paul writes that "the celebration of the Eucharist cannot be the starting-point for [ecclesial] communion; it presupposes that communion already exists, a communion which it seeks to consolidate and bring to perfection" (*Ecclesia de Eucharistia*, no. 35), we may still wonder whether John Paul has exhausted the ecumenical potential of the axiom of his long-ago predecessor Pope Innocent III—that the Eucharist "both signifies and effects ecclesiastical unity [*significat et efficit unitatem ecclesiasticam*]."[37] John Paul himself a little later in the encyclical puts the emphasis on the effective power of the Eucharist: "The Eucharist creates communion and fosters communion" (no. 40). The question therefore remains legitimate: How far do we have to be advanced in the unity which the celebration of the Eucharist "signifies" before we can draw on the sacramental grace to "effect" the fullness of that unity? Ongoing ecumenical exploration is appropriate in the determination and achievement both of what is required and what is sufficient for shared eucharistic communion to further ecclesial unity (*quod requiritur et sufficit*).

Ecumenically, "communion" has become in recent years perhaps the favorite ecclesiological category or model. In conjunction with the Second Vatican Council's relaunching of "communion ecclesiology," the Extraordinary Synod of Catholic Bishops in 1985 called communion "the central and fundamental idea of the Council's documents."[38] Here at least is what, in September 2001, Cardinal Joseph Ratzinger—then prefect of the Congregation for the Doctrine of the Faith—said in an address on "The Ecclesiology of Vatican II" at the opening of the pastoral congress of the diocese of Aversa (Italy):

Around the time of the Extraordinary Synod of 1985 which attempted to make an assessment of the 20 years since the Council there was a renewed effort to synthesize the Council's ecclesiology. The synthesis involved one basic concept: the ecclesiology of communion. I was very much pleased with this new focus in ecclesiology and I endeavored, to the extent I was able, to help work it out. First of all one must admit that the word "communio" did not occupy a central place in the Council. All the same, if properly understood it can serve as a synthesis of the essential elements of the Council's ecclesiology. All the essential elements of the Christian concept of "communio" can be found in the famous passage from the First Letter of Saint John (1:1-3); it is a frame of reference for the correct Christian understanding of "communio": "That which we have seen and heard we proclaim also to you, so that you may have fellowship (communio) with us; and our fellowship is with the Father and with his Son Jesus Christ. And we are writing this that our joy may be complete."[39]

To revert to my own ecclesial community, let me cite the very first paragraph of a recent British Methodist guide to the Lord's Supper, *Share This Feast: Reflecting on Holy Communion*:

Celebrating Holy Communion is always about participating in community. We gather together with other Christians, in the name of a God whose very nature is loving community—the Trinity. Communion is not something we can celebrate alone, and, though it always takes place in an actual human community, it isn't a feast that we create. It is something God offers and invites us to. We take our place alongside other people we know, whom we love and maybe struggle with, and in company with all faithful disciples, present and past, who celebrate across the world and before the face of God in heaven. We share as the "Body of Christ," the community of his followers.[40]

As to the discipline of admission to communion in the Methodist Church in Britain, that Church has a discipline of communion for its own members, and shows respect for the varied communion disciplines of other churches in quite a subtle way: "One of the keynotes of the Methodist revival was John Wesley's emphasis on 'The Duty of Constant Communion,' and it is still the duty and privilege of members of the Methodist Church to share in this sacrament. The Methodist Conference has encouraged local churches to admit baptized children to communion. Those who are communicants and belong to other Churches whose discipline so permits are also welcome as communicants in the Methodist Church."[41]

We might—one last time—open up the final horizon, where the communion we may expect to enjoy will be trinitarian in personal structure and cosmic in scope. Thus, at any rate, the conclusion of John Wesley's sermon "The New Creation": "And to crown all, there will be a deep, an intimate, an uninterrupted union with God; a constant communion with the Father and his Son Jesus Christ, through the Spirit, a continual enjoyment of the Three-One God, and of all creatures in him!"[42] And, just as we began the first lecture on "faith" with the Wesleyan "Spirit of faith, come down," so we may end this third lecture on "love" in unitedly praying even now for the deepening in ourselves of that Christic and ecclesial communion which will in its fullness characterize the End, and toward which "hope" already stretches. The Wesleyan hymn this time is "Christ, from whom all blessings flow":

Christ, from whom all blessings flow,
Perfecting the saints below,
Hear us, who Thy nature share,
Who Thy mystic body are.

Join us, in one spirit join,
Let us still receive of Thine;
Still for more on Thee we call,
Thou who fillest all in all.

Move, and actuate, and guide:
Divers gifts to each divide;
Placed according to Thy will,
Let us all our work fulfill;

Sweetly may we all agree,
Touched with loving sympathy:
Kindly for each other care;
Every member feel its share.

Love, like death, hath all destroyed,
Rendered all distinctions void;
Names, and sects, and parties fall:
Thou, O Christ, art all in all.[43]

NOTES
ॐ

1   *Unitatis Redintegratio*, I, 3. This document and others cited below are available on the Vatican's website at http://www.vatican.va.

2   This document and others cited below are available on the World Council of Churches' website at http://www.oikoumene.org.

3   Luis N. Rivera-Pagán, ed., *God in Your Grace . . . Official Report of the Ninth Assembly of the World Council of Churches* (Geneva: World Council of Churches Publications, 2007), 255–61, 276–77.

4   This precise hymn figured as no. 83 in the 1780 *Collection of Hymns for the Use of the People called Methodists*. It has retained its popularity in Methodism, and its use has spread well beyond.

5   World Council of Churches, *Baptism, Eucharist and Ministry*, Faith and Order Paper No. 111 (Geneva: World Council of Churches Publications, 1982). The document was quickly nicknamed *BEM*—no matter which of the many languages into which it was translated.

6   WCC, *Baptism, Eucharist and Ministry*: "Baptism," 11.

7   WCC, *Baptism, Eucharist and Ministry*: "Baptism," 17.

8   WCC, *Baptism, Eucharist and Ministry*: "Baptism," 8.

9   The text of John Wesley's "Letter to a Roman Catholic" may be found, for instance, in Albert Outler's anthology *John Wesley* (New York: Oxford University Press, 1964), 492–99. See also the ecumenical edition by Michael Hurley, S.J., *John Wesley's Letter to a Roman Catholic* (London and Dublin: Geoffrey Chapman, 1968).

10 See vol. 2 (ed. Albert C. Outler) in *The Works of John Wesley*, Bicentennial ed. (Nashville: Abingdon, 1985), 373–86, in particular p. 385. The passage quoted here is from sermon 55, paragraph 17.

11 Paul Fiddes, "Learning from Others: Baptists and Receptive Ecumenism," *Louvain Studies* 33 (2008): 54–73.

12 World Council of Churches, *Confessing the One Faith: An Ecumenical Explication of the Ecumenical Faith as It Is Confessed in the Nicene-Constantinopolitan Creed (381)*, Faith and Order Paper No. 153 (Geneva: World Council of Churches Publications, 1991). A recent collection of essays by various authors has been edited by the Baptist scholar Timothy George under the title *Evangelicals and Nicene Faith: Reclaiming the Apostolic Witness* (Grand Rapids: Baker Academic, 2011).

13 See World Council of Churches, *Baptism, Eucharist and Ministry 1982–1990: Report on the Process and Responses*, Faith and Order Paper No. 149 (Geneva: World Council of Churches Publications, 1990), 112.

14 Thomas F. Best, ed., *Baptism Today: Understanding, Practice, Ecumenical Implications*, Faith and Order Paper No. 207 (Collegeville, Minn.: Liturgical Press, 2008).

15 World Council of Churches, *One Baptism: Towards Mutual Recognition*, Faith and Order Paper No. 210 (Geneva: World Council of Churches Publications, 2011).

16 World Council of Churches, *Eighth Report of the Joint Working Group between the Roman Catholic Church and the World Council of Churches* (Geneva: World Council of Churches Publications, 2005), 45–72.

17 Raymond Brown's essay is found in his *New Testament Essays* (New York: Paulist Press, 1963), 217–53.

18 Brown, *New Testament Essays*, 226–27.

19 Brown, *New Testament Essays*, 226 n. 25.

20 Lesslie Newbigin, *Signs amid the Rubble: The Purposes of God in Human History*, ed. and intro. Geoffrey Wainwright (Grand Rapids: Eerdmans, 2003), 47.

21 Originally published by Epworth Press (London, 1971), *Eucharist and Eschatology* underwent several expanded editions (New York: Oxford University Press, 1981; Akron, Ohio: Order of St. Luke Publications, 2002; Peterborough, England: Epworth Press, 2003).

22 Brown, *New Testament Essays*, 248.

23 Brown, *New Testament Essays*, 248–53.

24 See, for instance, T. W. Manson, "The Lord's Prayer," *Bulletin of the John Rylands Library of Manchester* 38, no. 1 (1955): 99–113.

25 Latin text with facing-page French translation is found in Michel Réveillaud, *Saint Cyprien: L'Oraison dominicale: Texte, traduction, introduction et notes* (Paris: Presses Universitaires de France, 1964).

26 World Council of Churches, *Sharing in One Hope: Reports and Documents from the Meeting of the Faith and Order Commission, Bangalore 1978*, Faith and Order Paper No. 92 (Geneva: World Council of Churches Publications, 1979); see in particular pp. 195–202.

27 *Unitatis Redintegratio*, 1, 4.

28 *Ut Unum Sint*, nos. 83–84.

29 Appearing first in Charles Wesley's "Funeral Hymns" of 1759, this hymn was omitted from the 1780 *Collection of Hymns for the Use of the People Called Methodists*, but it began to appear in the *Supplement* of 1831 and has kept its place in Methodist usage.

30 "Constitution on the Sacred Liturgy," *Sacrosanctum Concilium*, 47, following St. Augustine (*Tractatus in Ioannis Evangelium*, 6:13) and St. Thomas Aquinas (*Summa Theologiae* III.73, a.3).

31 See *The Book of Offices, authorized for use in the Methodist Church* (London: Methodist Publishing House, 1936). The forms of service are stated to have been authorized for use by the Conference of the Methodist Church at Newcastle-on-Tyne in July 1936. The various printings in 1936 and later always contained "The Lord's Supper, or Holy Communion."

32 WCC, *Baptism, Eucharist and Ministry*: "Eucharist," 2.

33 WCC, *Baptism, Eucharist and Ministry*: "Eucharist," 29.

34 For what immediately follows, see my article "Intercommunion," in Nicholas Lossky et al., eds., *Dictionary of the Ecumenical Movement*, 2nd ed. (Geneva: World Council of Churches Publications, 2002), 586–89.

35 T. F. Torrance, "Eschatology and the Eucharist," in *Intercommunion*, ed. D. Baillie and J. Marsh (London: SCM Press, 1952), 303–50, in particular p. 304.

36 *Orientalium Ecclesiarum*, nos. 26–29; *Ecumenical Directory*, 1967, nos. 39–45; *Ecumenical Directory*, 1993, nos. 122–28.

37 *De sacro altaris mysterio*, IV, 36; PL 217:879.

38 See the theological work of Jean-Marie R. Tillard, O.P., *Église d'églises: L'ecclésiologie de communion* (Paris: Éditions du Cerf, 1987), also published as *Church of Churches: The Ecclesiology of Communion* (Collegeville, Minn.: Liturgical Press, 1992); and for a survey of other preparatory and subsequent work in modern theology, see Dennis M. Doyle, *Communion Ecclesiology: Visions and Versions* (Maryknoll, N.Y.: Orbis Books, 2000).

39 "The Ecclesiology of Vatican II." The Cathedral Foundation, *L'Osservatore Romano*, English ed. (Baltimore, Md.), January 23, 2002, page 5. See https://www.ewtn.com/library/curia/cdfeccv2.htm.

40 As of 2006, the booklet was available from the Methodist Publishing House, Peterborough, England, 2006; cited here from page 6.

41 *The Methodist Worship Book* (Peterborough, England: Methodist Publishing House, 1999), 114.

42 See vol. 2 in *The Works of John Wesley* (as in note 10 above), 510.

43 This hymn of Charles Wesley—sometimes in variant form—has figured regularly in Methodist hymnals since the 1780 *Collection of Hymns for the Use of the People called Methodists*, where it was numbered 504.

CPSIA information can be obtained at www.ICGtesting.com
Printed in the USA
BVOW07s0345230614

356993BV00001B/1/P